JUDITH G. WOLF
TIDBITS TOO

Judith G. Wolf

2   Acknowledgement

Another huge thank you to George Susich, Creative Director at Susich Design Co. for putting this book together, to Alicia Keenon who has faithfully read all of my poetry and made many helpful suggestions and corrections, and to my proofreaders, Lee Ann Grace, Alicia Keenon and Erin Sandmann.

Cover / Book Design: Susich Design Co, Phoenx AZ
Cover Image: Chris Loomis
ISBN: 978-0-9967860-4-1

Judith G. Wolf, Ph.D. is a poet and artist. A Buffalo, New York native and long time resident of Phoenix Arizona, her published poetry collections include *Weeping Shadows, Tidbits, Otherwise* and *I Hate Being in Love Alone.*

A number of Dr. Wolf's writings have been set to music, including 12 compositions from *Otherwise* that were included in a work titled "Poems of Life." It was created by the noted composer Kenneth Fuchs and premiered with the Virginia Symphony Orchestra in 2017. "Poems of Life" was also recorded at Abbey Road with the London Philharmonic as part of a four-selection recording of Fuchs' music, and it won a coveted Grammy Award in the Classical Compendium category in 2019.

Dr. Wolf's poem "Fresh Grief" was put to music by Michael Lewis and premiered in Chandler, Arizona in 2018. A variety of her other writings have also been set to music: Clint Borzoni and *Tidbits* (premiered in Belvedere, California in 2017), Mason Bates and *Afterlife* (premiered with the Phoenix Symphony in 2013), and Persis Vehar and *Life, Love, Timelessness,* which featured six of Dr. Wolf's poems (written for the professional Music Teachers of New Mexico, premiered in 2012).

A creative arts advocate, Dr. Wolf founded Arizona Spark, which supports the development and production of new and innovative

4   operatic works for Arizona Opera. Additionally, she co-founded the Phoenix Symphony Commissioning Club, which commissioned new compositions by four noteworthy composers, including Daron Hagen and Kenneth Fuchs.

Notably, Dr. Wolf also co-founded and is President/CEO of Young Arts Arizona Ltd., a nonprofit art organization that serves at-risk children by exhibiting their artwork and teaching art to underserved children in medical facilities. She holds a Doctor of Ministry through the Universal Life Church and is a Reiki Master. Additionally, Dr. Wolf is an Honorary Commander with the 944th Fighter Wing at Luke Air Force Base.

Dr. Wolf's diverse educational and professional background includes a Ph.D. in Educational Psychology, a Master's degree in Elementary and Remedial Education, and extensive experience in arts administration. She also serves on several Boards of Directors, including Arizona Opera and the Metropolitan Opera National Council Auditions, Arizona District.

For complete information see: www.judithgwolf.com

PREFACE

Come Ons

Would you like to bundle?

I don't seem to turn you on so I dressed down.

Most people look better in clothes. Should we check?

Want me to read you a bedtime story?

I can't sleep at night. I'm not used to sleeping alone.

Want to have a sleepover?

I would jump all over you but I don't like to be rejected.

If you wore a kilt you would be more accessible.

I never know when it's going to happen so I wear
fancy pants every day just in case.

If you want me to seduce you you'll have to give me
more to drink.

Are we going to have a platonic relationship or
should we try fooling around and see if it works?

Let's consummate our friendship.

Should I start the foreplay now or put it on hold?

JUDITH G. WOLF
TIDBITS TOO

How does a rainbow taste?   7

8   Joyful singing
seeps onto
the paper
of life.

I no longer care
what you think
of me.
You died
and set
me free.

10   Time to go.
My hearing aids
are tired.

Merrily we roll
along
roll
along
roll along.
Merrily
we
roll
along.
OOPS.

12   I am in love
with an
illusion.

Love is like
the ocean—
deep ends
shallow ends.

Lonely locust
sitting by my car in a
parking lot
near a grocery store.
W.A.I.T.I.N.G.
While
I
sit wondering
when to
back up.

Old people
fart a lot.
Get used to it.
We're living longer.

I think I work so
much to avoid life.
When mine is over
I will have totally
missed it.

Burning joy
singes my soul.
Bliss blasting outward
projects hyperboles.

18 Waiting for this
meeting is like
waiting to see what
life after death
is like.

Oh right!
I am
going
to
die.
I keep
forgetting.

20

Sorry I'm late.
I didn't know
where to
put my
eyebrows.

Fund raising etiquette:
No need
to thank
a bequest
once it's
been
received.

The meaning of
importance is
showing my new book
to a friend
WHO
reads it quietly
and googles
her Facebook page.

A million is
a millisecond
of existence.

24

He died,
I didn't.
Fill in the
blank_____.

I think I'll wear
all black with a red
jacket – then I'm
covered for
any occasion.

A giant Deja vu...
flash
splash
squash.

Each night I dream
of you and wonder why
we never met.

Even though I may not
be sure there is a God
He is still taking really
good care of me.

You have the life
I wanted but
couldn't have.

30

Soon the day
will end
the date
will change
but
I will
NOT.

The memories
were more
wonderful
than the
actuality.

32

Strange
to think of
a world out
there
without
me
in it.

It's best
not to bring
out the bitch
in people.

34   A bubble
            of doubt.

Years of
Saturdays
pass by.

If egos would
leave the scene
we might reach
a higher good.

I can't live my
life afraid
of how I
am going
to die.

I have so many
doctors I even
have one for my
middle finger.

Picking your nose in the
car is a solitary activity.

40

The movie was
a metaphor
for life.
Everyone died.

He is so commitment
phobic you can't say
any word beginning with
L   life love longing lettuce.

42

When I met my
father-in-law he
told me he was
going to die at 60.
He lived to just short
of 100.
I always wonder how he
managed the last 40 years.

I wanted to impress you so
I wore eye makeup.

44

It tastes like
cherry pop with
bad breath.

I am giving you a
fart for Christmas.
You don't seem
to have any.

46   I have a friend who
squeezes the love
out of you.

What is life-
a walk in the park,
a drink before dinner.

Reaching nirvana is
simply living long enough
to outlast your
disapproving
friends
and relatives.

While looking for the
fountain of youth
I found...

If you are
claustrophobic
don't wish
for immortality.
Could get crowded.

If we live forever
when will we
meet God?

A bird wee-weed on me
and I thought it was raining.

The purpose
of grief
is humility.

54   What does
      it hurt
      to believe.

I keep wondering
which persona
to wear.

I thought of you this
morning while I was
cleaning out the
coffee pot.

I am full of
poems and every
once in a while
I vomit one up.

58 You are the coal
in my stocking.

If you want

a happy ending

read a romance novel.

60

On my deathbed
I hope I can sing
like Puccini's Mimi.

Power surges off
the dollar bill causing
hurricanes.

I was walking
along and
fell in a hole.
You sealed it
with a sewer
cover.

Step out of yourself
and talk to me.

You are the
only member
of this team.

When the title says it all
the poem goes unwritten.

66   You put a governor
on my mouth.

Where did the birds hang
out before there were
telephone wires?

68   If you're going to criticize the
            universe, remember that you are in it.

I've been cooked too long.
Not turned over even once.

The clown
sang alone.

Women like a relationship
like they read about in books
or hear about in songs...
you know, someone
fawning over them.

Food today
is over the top.
The next thing
you'll see
is arugula and
grape nut
flake cereal.

My voice
sounds like
a piano that
needs to be
tuned.

I'm walking around
taking a nap.

Life is a painting.
If you craft it
correctly it
might turn
out with
depth.

Don't project your psychopathology onto your friends.

For a minute there I thought I loved you.

He and she are so
good together.
Too bad he's gay.

I don't feel very well
but I bet if you tell me
you love me, I will recover
quickly.

I'm so nice that if you displease me you'll probably never know.

Be who you are.
Don't act out
your insecurities.

God doesn't care what you wear.

I don't like being
in love all alone.

Problem is we are tripping
over each other's insecurities.

I am from New York State.
I am direct. I will kiss your
ass when you deserve it.

Getting old is like falling off
a cliff in slow motion.

Martini Mistake
Snitch
Glitch
Fuck.

Anticipation of a fun
event is really fun.

Wearing mascara
every day is making my
eyelashes tired.

90

New love is a pain in the ass.
Ecstatic one minute,
despondent the next.
Where have you been all week.

I can't smile.
I'm eating spinach.

Don't fall in love with someone unless you are sure they are in love with you first.

It's easy to misunderstand silence.   93

I think I am highly amusing.
Either that or cry.

I got my hearing test
prescription from my
gynecologist.

Zero amount of food
has the lowest amount
of calories.

I know what I mean.

How come you don't?

You are so divine I want
to marry you. We will live in
Utah - husband husband wife.
Who will cook?

You either care or you don't care.
Sorta care doesn't work.

100   Life is a long fuse burning quicker than expected.

I think I'll wear hot pink underwear,
that way I will know I'm sexy even
if no one else does.

102   A text does not fill the silence.

I absolutely adore you.

If you absolutely adore me,

we can meet in the middle.

104   A finger intruded into my life and flicked off a word.

www.ingramcontent.com/pod-product-compliance
Lightning Source LLC
Chambersburg PA
CBHW071234090426
42736CB00014B/3080